W9-CJS-175

PICTURE HISTORY

TRANSPORT

IN HISTORY

Alan Blackwood

4239513

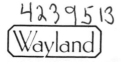

PICTURE HISTORY

CLOTHES   MEDICINE
EXPLORATION   RECREATION
FARMING   RELIGION
FOOD   SCHOOLS
HOMES   SHOPPING
LANDSCAPE   TRANSPORT
MACHINES   WARFARE

First published in 1984 by
Wayland (Publishers) Limited
49 Lansdowne Place, Hove
East Sussex BN3 1HF, England

© Copyright 1984 Wayland (Publishers) Ltd

ISBN 0 85078 354 2

Series Design by Behram Kapadia

Phototypeset by Direct Image, Hove
Printed in Italy by G. Canale & C.S.p.A., Turin
Bound in the U.K. by The Pitman Press, Bath

Contents

448924

Introduction

Can you imagine what it would be like never to move more than a short distance away from the place where you were born? Until about two hundred years ago, that was the situation for most people. Only the rich and powerful travelled in the normal course of their lives. The rest stayed put, working on farms, or at some local trade or craft. When they moved at all, it was probably on their own two feet. There were no cars, buses or trains, and you had to be wealthy just to own a horse.

How that situation quickly and dramatically changed is told in this book. In words and pictures, it marks the progress from stage coach (at a time when nobody had ever travelled faster than the speed of a horse) to supersonic jet and space-craft.

Transport of Goods

Passenger travel is only part of the story. People may not have travelled widely until recent times, but the transport of goods has always played a vital part in human affairs. In these pages we can see and read about the galleys that plied up and down the Nile in the far-off days of the pharaohs; the camel caravans that crossed deserts and mountains; the sailing ships, steam boats, barges, trains and trucks, aircraft and helicopters, that have kept the wheels of trade and commerce rolling from ancient times to the present day.

Pioneers

What has transport meant to the world's explorers and pioneers? Think of the Phoenicians, who may have been the first people to sail out into the unknown waters of the Atlantic; of the voyages of Columbus and Vasco da Gama; of the wagon trains and railroads that opened up America's Wild West; of Louis Blériot, first man to fly the Channel between England and France, and Charles Lindbergh, first to fly solo across the Atlantic; of Yuri Gagarin, first man in space, and Neil Armstrong, first man to step on to the Moon; of space probes to Venus and Mars. They are all featured here.

So are many of the great engineers and inventors who have helped to make it all possible: Thomas Telford, John MacAdam, the Montgolfier Brothers, Henri Giffard, George and Robert Stephenson, Isambard Kingdom Brunel, Karl Benz, the Wright Brothers, Graf von Zeppelin, Frank Whittle.

The whole fascinating story of transport in our world throughout the ages, and of how we have now learnt to travel beyond it, is vividly recounted and illustrated within the covers of this book.

Alan Blackwood was an editor of children's books before becoming a freelance author. Among the books he has written are *The Pageant of Music* and *The Performing World of the Singer*. He is also the author of *Recreation in History*, and *Religion in History*, in this series.

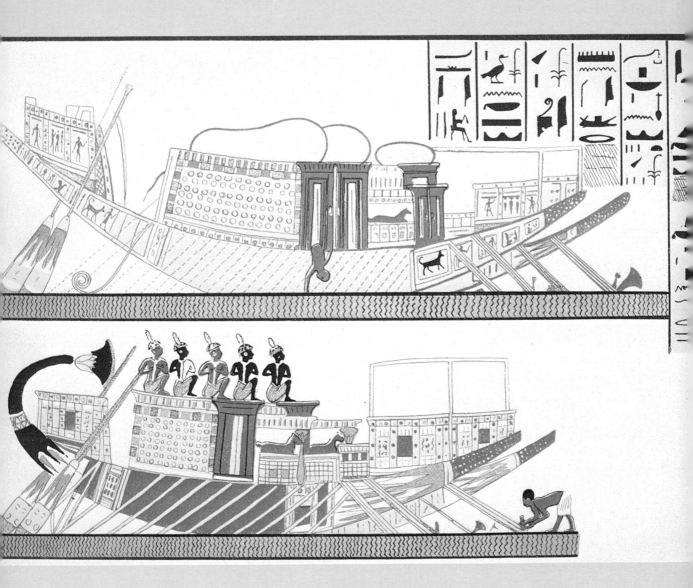

By River and Sea

The boats depicted in this Egyptian wall painting, or mural, plied up and down the River Nile four thousand years ago. Most early civilizations grew up along the banks of a great river, one reason being that river transport was usually more efficient than transport over land. Boats were easier to handle and could take greater loads than a beast of burden or a heavy ox cart.

River Highway

The Egyptians used the Nile for almost all their travel and transport. They even had special barges for the dead. The boats shown here were probably built from planks of acacia wood, and were about 18 metres (60 ft) long. The top boat, loaded with bales of cotton, may have used paddles. The lower one, carrying passengers, had oars. Both were steered by the large decorated paddles at the stern.

The largest Egyptian vessels measured up to 56 metres (180 ft) in length. As well as oars, they had a mast and sail that could be raised or lowered as required. Travelling southward down the Nile, and against the current, the crew raised their sail to take advantage of the north wind blowing down the Nile valley. Returning northward, they furled the sail, lowered the mast, and went along with the current. This practice was so much a part of Egyptian life that in their written hieroglyphics (there are some included in our picture) the image or symbol meaning 'go south' was a boat with a sail, while that for 'go north' was a boat without one.

The Egyptians also sailed round the eastern Mediterranean coast, and down the Red Sea and beyond to a part of East Africa that they called the Land of Punt. There is an account of an expedition to the Land of Punt that returned with a cargo of monkeys and apes, animal hides and slaves.

The Phoenicians

The greatest sailors of the ancient world were probably the Phoenicians. Their homeland was the coastal region around the city of Tyre, now Lebanon. From about 800 to 600 BC, the Phoenicians sailed the length and breadth of the Mediterranean, trading in every commodity of the time: timber, wheat, oil, wine, papyrus, cotton, ivory, pottery, bronze- and copper-ware, gems and jewellery, spices and perfumes. They sailed on into the Atlantic — perhaps the first sailors to navigate out of sight of land — reaching such far-flung places as the Canary Isles and southern Britain.

Phoenician ships, like Egyptian ones, were galleys — long, narrow vessels equipped with oars and sail. The Greeks and Romans, in their turn, built galleys for trade and war. These were called biremes or triremes, depending on whether they had two or three rows or banks of oarsmen to give them extra power and speed.

la requeste con
templacion et
plaisance de
treshault e no
ble prince mo

Jehan froissart prestre e cha
rellain a mon treschier seigr
deffuts nomme. Et pour le
temps de lors tresorier e cha
nome de chimay et de lille

Horse-drawn Vehicles

This illustration is from a medieval 'illuminated' manuscript. A lady, perhaps a queen or princess, is being carried along in a horse-drawn litter. Her attendant ladies-in-waiting follow on horseback. Important-looking ministers surround her and a mounted guard of honour is drawn up by the city gate. You had to be an important person to travel at all in the Middle Ages.

For Ladies Only!

A litter was the name for any sort of wheel-less vehicle, with poles at each end, transported either by horses or by men. The elegant sedan chair (named after the town in eastern France), borne along by footmen, was a special kind of litter of a later age.

In medieval times there were also passenger wagons, or whirlicotes. These were fancy versions of the rough old ox carts that carried agricultural produce from the fields or transported heavy equipment in times of war. They usually had a wooden frame supporting a decorated canvas awning, but the bodywork still rested directly on the axles, so giving a very bumpy ride. Litters and whirlicotes, it should be added, were for ladies only. Men either walked everywhere or rode about on horseback.

The situation changed in Renaissance times (that is, from about the year 1450). A new form of horse-drawn vehicle, better constructed than the medieval wagons, with a proper roof instead of an awning, began to appear. It was called a 'coach', after a town in Hungary named Kocs, where some of the very first examples were built.

Elizabeth I was the first English monarch to travel about regularly in one of the new-style coaches. Her French counterpart, Henri IV, had a splendid coach built for him, with a decorated canopy, curtains all round, and four wheels protected by what we would nowadays call mudguards.

More Comfort

During the seventeenth century, coaches were made much more comfortable. They were fitted with glass windows instead of leather curtains, and the body of the coach was suspended between the wheels by leather straps for an easier ride. These were the types of coach that such monarchs as Charles II of England and Louis XIV of France travelled in.

Most luxurious of all were such famous ceremonial coaches as the one built in 1757 for the Lord Mayor of London — which still appears each year in the Lord Mayor's Show. Coaches like this looked very grand, but were covered with so much ornamental carving and other decorations that they could move only at a snail's pace.

By that time, as we can read on page 23, much faster, better-designed coaches, available to all classes of people, were coming on to the roads.

Wind Power

This is how an artist depicted English soldiers embarking for France to fight in the Hundred Years War — the long struggle between the kings of England and France between 1338 to 1453.

The ships make an interesting comparison with those on pages 9 and 27. They are much wider than the old Egyptian or Phoenician galleys, providing more space in a shorter length. They are not galleys but true sailing ships. Their sail is much larger in relation to their size and bulk than the sail on a galley. The extra wind power meant that oarsmen were not needed. This left more space for cargo and for passengers.

You can see that these ships have rudders, attached by a kind of hinge to the centre of the stern. Ships carrying greater weights of cargo, and borne along by the power of larger sails, needed more efficient steering gear than the galleys to control their direction.

Trading Ships

Sailing ships of this general design were called cogs. They handled most sea traffic across the English Channel and North Sea and through to the Baltic Sea during the later Middle Ages (from about 1200 to 1400).

Many cogs had square, castle-like structures added to bow and stern, as a defence against pirates. Pirates were the menace that first made sea traders in northern Europe team up in a kind of federation called the Hanseatic League (from the old German word *Hansa*, meaning 'company'). The League was based on the German sea ports of Bremen, Hamburg and Lübeck, and Cologne on the River Rhine. From small beginnings, the Hanseatic League became an international organization controlling sea trade from London all the way to Riga on the Baltic coast and on, overland, to Novgorod in Russia.

Carracks and Caravels

During the fifteenth century, cogs began to be replaced by larger ships with two or three masts, and sails that could more easily be adjusted to changing weather conditions. It was in these new types of sailing ship, called carracks and caravels, that Christopher Columbus and Vasco da Gama made their voyages of discovery, to America and round the African coast to India.

Such voyages opened up great new trade routes between Europe and the rest of the world. In Central and South America, especially, Spanish explorers discovered huge quantities of gold. They built larger ships still, with two or three sails on each mast, to transport the heavy gold back across the Atlantic to Spain.

It was these Spanish galleons that Sir Francis Drake attacked, both on the high seas and as they sailed up the Channel in 1588, as part of the great Armada sent to invade England.

وَسُكْنَى وَمُسْكِنِي وَجُزْءٍ وَجَانِي ، وَمَآبِي وَمَالِي ، وَلَا تَجْعَلْنِي لِنَفْسِي

سُلْطَانًا عَلَى غَيْرِي ، وَاجْعَلْ مِنْ لَدُنْكَ سُلْطَانًا نَصِيرًا   اللَّهُمَّ اجْرُسْنِي بِعَيْنِكَ وَبِرُكْنِكَ   وَلَا

وَاحْفَظْنِي يَا مَنِيكَ وَمِنْكَ ، وَتَوَلَّنِي بِأَخْبَارِكَ وَخَيْرِكَ   وَلَا تَكِلْنِي إِلَى كَلَاءَةٍ غَيْرِكَ

وَمَتِّعْنِي بِعَافِيَةٍ غَيْرِ عَافِيَةٍ   وَارْزُقْنِي رَفَاهِيَّةً غَيْرَ رَفَاهِيَةٍ   وَاكْفِنِي مَآثِمَ الْأَوَاءَ

Across the Desert

This Arabian 'miniature', painted over 700 years ago, shows a caravan, or camel train, on the move. Caravans represent one of the most ancient forms of transport on land. The Old Testament of the Bible mentions them several times.

As we have read on page 9, the earliest civilizations grew up along the banks of a river. But they were often separated from each other by great tracts of desert. Communication and trade between groups of people relied to a large extent on a remarkable animal — the camel. Its broad, strong feet kept it plodding along over the roughest terrain; it could go for weeks without fresh food or water, thanks to the fat stored in its hump; and it could carry up to 270 kilograms (600 lbs) of stores or merchandise.

Camel Caravans

Even with so sturdy a beast, nobody would dream of crossing a desert on their own, where to be stranded almost certainly meant death. So merchants and other travellers teamed up with their camels to form a convoy or caravan — from the Persian word *karvan*, meaning a crowd of people. Before they started out, they usually chose a leader from amongst themselves — a *karvan-bashi* or caravan chief — to take decisions and settle any disputes that might arise. Then the caravan set off.

Real caravans would not have presented such a pretty sight as our picture: just a long line of men and beasts slowly winding their way between barren, rocky hills, or on and on across shifting dunes of sand. On a good day they might make 35 kilometres (about 20 miles). Spring and autumn were the best times of year for the caravans, when it was neither too hot nor too cold. Even then, a caravan might be held up for days by high winds that whipped the sand into stinging, blinding clouds. Most caravans took weeks, perhaps months, to complete their journey.

Overland Routes

One of the ancient caravan routes, bringing precious ivory from tropical Africa to the Mediterranean Sea, ran across the Sahara from Timbuktu and the River Niger to Tripoli on the North African coast. Another, even longer route was across the steppes of Central Asia and the huge, empty Gobi desert to China, a distance of 5,000 kilometres (3,000 miles). Marco Polo used this route on his epic journey in 1274 to the court of Kublai Khan in Peking.

The great caravan routes of Africa and Asia were vitally important for thousands of years. Only with the coming of railways, and later, air transport, have they become a thing of the past. But monuments to them remain; caravanserai — fortress-like buildings on the outskirts of towns in the Middle East, that offered shelter to the men and beasts of the long and lonely caravans.

Island Voyage

This vivid painting of a Tahitian war canoe putting to sea shows a local chief, in gorgeous head-dress, standing in the stern. Totem poles are fastened to the bow.

Tahiti belongs to the group of islands known collectively as Polynesia (the name itself means 'many islands') that are scattered over the Pacific Ocean in an area two or three times as large as the whole of Europe. Naturally, the sea is of prime importance to the peoples of Polynesia. Fish is their staple diet; and until this century, the only means of transport and communication between them was by sea.

The islanders used canoes for fishing and for ceremonial displays, but they built rafts for the more serious business of ocean crossing. Rafts are one of the most stable types of boat, since they lie flat on the surface of the sea and run little risk of capsizing. Polynesian rafts usually had a hut lashed to the deck and carried a sail.

What has intrigued historians is how, in time's past, the sailors of Polynesia managed to find their way between islands, often huge distances apart, without such aids as maps or a compass.

Following the Stars

It is a fascinating story. During the day, they were guided by the sun. But they also had a good knowledge of astronomy. They plotted the stars, distinguishing between the 'fixed stars' and 'wandering stars' (planets). Thus, by night they read the heavens, following patterns or groups of stars that led them to a thousand different islands.

Even without sun or stars, they were not lost. They knew where the ocean currents would carry them. The shape, shade and behaviour of clouds also gave them valuable clues about how far they were from land.

Thor Heyerdahl

The most celebrated scholar of Polynesian culture has been the Norwegian Thor Heyerdahl. He believed the islands of Polynesia may originally have been colonized by people from South America who sailed across the Pacific, using the ocean currents to help them.

In 1947, to prove his point, he constructed a raft measuring 14 metres (45 ft) by 5.6 metres (18 ft), with a hut and sail. He named it *Kon-Tiki*, after an ancient Inca chieftain, and with two companions, he set sail from the coast of Peru. They made a westerly crossing of 7,000 kilometres, (nearly 4,400 miles) to the lonely Pacific island of Raroia in 101 days.

In 1970 Thor Heyerdahl crossed the Atlantic in another type of raft, called *Ra*, made from reeds. He made this voyage to support his belief that the ancient Egyptians might have sailed to the Americas five or six thousand years ago.

Overland to the West

This attractive picture of travel in America's Wild West in the 1860s shows a wagon train proceeding along a broad green valley, with the Rocky Mountains rising majestically behind. Two friendly Red Indians on horseback watch its progress.

But it was not always like this for pioneer Americans on the move. Here is an entry from the diary of one of them: 'At 7.30 we found our encampment near the creek, having travelled fourteen miles in thirteen hours. There is but little grass here and a poor chance for cattle. . . The creek is so very steep as to be almost impossible for heavy wagons to ascend, and so narrow that the least accident might precipitate a wagon down a bank three or four hundred feet, in which case it would certainly be dashed to pieces . . .'

The Mormons

These words were written by a Mormon. The Mormons were a religious sect who wanted to found their own community. In 1847 they set out from Illinois westward across the Mississippi, then on over the prairies and into the Rocky Mountains as far as the Great Salt Lake in Utah territory — a distance of 2,500 kilometres (1,500 miles).

Men, women and children travelled by covered wagon. Each wagon carried, besides passengers, about 3,000 kilograms (3 tons) of stores and equipment, and needed up to twelve oxen, yoked together in pairs,

to haul it.

Looking after the cattle was one of the pioneers' biggest concerns. Each evening the wagon train halted and the wagons were drawn up into large circles. The gaps between them were closed with fencing, to create a large pen, within which the cattle were grazed, rested and groomed.

As our diarist records, the wagon trains were often on the move for thirteen or fourteen hours each day, depending on the time of year. The seasons affected travel in other important ways. In summer, the hooves of the cattle, pounding along the same narrow track, often raised clouds of choking dust. With the onset of winter there was rain and mud, then snow, with the threat that the wagon train might be trapped in drifts for days or weeks on end.

The Boer Trekkers

Another epic trek was made by Dutch settlers in South Africa in the years 1834 to 1838. These Boers (farmers) and their families wished to separate from the British in Cape Colony. About ten thousand of them, in their wagons, made the 1,400-kilometre (900-mile) journey across the Orange and Vaal rivers, to settle in the region now called the Transvaal. As they moved northward towards the equator, the land became increasingly hot and barren. But they would not turn back. In those days no one travelled for fun.

A MIDNIGHT RACE ON THE MISSISSIPPI.

River Highways

A Midnight Race on the Mississippi is the title of this 1860 print. To judge by the showers of sparks flying out of their funnels, both boats are in danger of catching fire or blowing up, in their eagerness to be first. In fact, daredevil races like this did sometimes end in calamity.

As we have read on page 9, rivers were probably the setting for the earliest of all forms of transportation and they still provide us with some of the biggest contrasts in the whole area of transport and travel. Distinctive sailing boats like the Egyptian dhow or felucca, and the Chinese junk, continue to ply the waters of the Nile and the Yangtse-kiang rivers, as they have for centuries. Compare them with the huge rafts of logs guided by lumberjacks down swirling rivers from forest to timber mill in Canada, Scandinavia and northern Russia. Then again, think of the Rhine, with its teeming barge traffic between Germany's industrial Ruhr and Rotterdam, the world's busiest port, by the North Sea.

No one could mistake the steamboats in our picture as belonging to any other river but the Mississippi. Because of the way they were built, with broad hull and high superstructure, they made ideal pleasure craft. But during the years when the United States was developing into one of the world's richest nations, these distinctive boats had a much more important role to play than pleasure.

The Mississippi

The Mississippi, with its main tributary the Missouri, flows north to south for over 6,000 kilometres (3,800 miles), through some of the nation's richest farmlands, and on to the Gulf of Mexico. First barges, and later the celebrated steamboats, carried grain, cotton and tobacco from loading points along the river to the port of New Orleans, for export around the world.

The old riverboats are now only colourful reminders of the past. Today big diesel-powered barges and tankers carry on the real business of America's great waterway.

The Volga

Another mighty river with a colourful history is the Volga, flowing for 3,500 kilometres (2,300 miles) south-eastward from Russia's forests and snows to the semi-desert lands around the Caspian Sea. 'Mother Volga', as the Russians call it, has for centuries served as a main artery of communication and transport. In the Middle Ages it was also one of the most important travel routes between Europe and Asia.

At one time teams of serfs carried boats overland from one navigable stretch of river to the next, or hauled boats upsteam against the flow of the current. The famous 'Volga Boat Song' commemorates this.

Today the Volga is linked by canal to Moscow, Archangel and the Baltic, and still handles a great deal of heavy goods traffic.

Coach and Horses

Road travel before the days of the car was often very uncomfortable. This early nineteenth-century mail coach is caught in a thunderstorm. The horses rear up in fright and the driver and his companions hold on to their hats in the wind and rain.

Horse-drawn coaches, offering a public passenger service, first appeared about 1600. Known as stage wagons, because at appointed stages of the journey the horses were changed, they trundled along at about six kilometres an hour (4 m.p.h.). They were, nonetheless, a wonderful new way of getting about for those not rich enough to afford a coach or even a horse of their own.

actual stage coach — run mainly for passengers. The other was the mail coach, sponsored by the government, for providing a speedy postal service between London and other large cities. Mail coaches did not take as many passengers as a stage coach, they often ran during the night, and their fares were expensive. But with their smart black, maroon and red colours, like the one in our picture, they were the fastest, most stylish form of public transport on the roads. With frequent changes of horses at staging posts, they could maintain a speed of nearly 20 km/h (12 m.p.h.), which in those days was very good going indeed.

Better Roads

Not much was done to improve upon the lumbering old stage wagons while most roads remained little better than cart tracks. But during the eighteenth century, thanks to the work of engineers like John Metcalf, John MacAdam and Thomas Telford, roads were much improved. So coaches could be built with light but stronger wheels, free-moving front axles, and suspension belts and springs, for greater speed, better steering and a more comfortable ride.

These developments were especially noticeable in Britain, because the relatively short distances between towns and generally easy terrain favoured such transport.

By 1800 there were two types of coach operating on Britain's roads. One was the

Status Symbols

All this activity sparked off a fashion for even better appointed, 'dashing' private coaches and open carriages. Models like the Brougham, Landau and Phaeton were status symbols, in the same way as different types of cars were to be for later generations. There was also the jaunty, two-wheeled Hansom cab, one of the most familiar sights in nineteenth-century London.

There were some distinctive American coaches too, notably the Buggy, and the Surrey, which had a special kind of fringed canopy over the seats.

But they were all to vanish from the roads before the end of the nineteenth century, as first railways and then motor cars appeared on the scene.

24

Commercial Waterways

Here is a busy scene on the Regent's Canal in London around the year 1820. Before the coming of the railways (see page 29), canals handled much of Britain's growing industrial traffic.

The first of these industrial waterways was the Bridgewater Canal, opened in 1761. It linked a coal mine owned by the Duke of Bridgewater with Manchester. By the time of our picture, about 5,000 kilometres (3,000 miles) of canal linked Britain's new factories and fast-growing towns and cities. The two barges in the picture come from Manchester. They have probably brought cotton goods from the Lancashire mills to London. One of the barges is being hauled by two men and a horse waits to pull another. Barges were not mechanized in those days.

Building Canals

Canal building itself was not a simple matter of cutting a channel through the countryside. Unlike a road, which can carry traffic up and down hills without much trouble, a canal must be dead level. Famous engineers, such as James Brindley and Thomas Telford, tackled this problem in several ways.

Over stretches where the gradient was not too steep, they regulated the canal level by locks, like the one pictured here. By opening and closing the gates the locks raised or lowered the barges from one water level to another. Where a canal encountered hills or valleys, it had to go through tunnels or over special bridges called aqueducts.

Vital Links

Railways and then roads have taken most of the traffic away from the old canals of countries like Britain and France. But in many other countries, much larger canals, connecting inland towns and cities with the sea, are still vitally important. The St Lawrence Seaway in North America is a system of canals and locks extending for 3,000 kilometres (1,900 miles) along the length of the St Lawrence river, so opening up the whole area of the Great Lakes to shipping from the Atlantic ocean.

Other canals connect oceans and seas. The Suez Canal, opened in 1869, was the work of the French engineer Ferdinand de Lesseps. By providing a direct link for shipping between the Mediterranean and Red Seas, it cut the distance of the sea route between Europe and the Far East by nearly 10,000 kilometres (6,000 miles).

In 1881 de Lesseps also planned a canal through the isthmus of Panama, linking the Atlantic and Pacific oceans, so saving ships the voyage down the length of South America and round Cape Horn. The Panama Canal was opened in 1914 — an 80-kilometre (50-mile) waterway, with 12 mechanically-operated locks, capable of handling large ships. Over 15,000 ships still pass through this famous canal each year.

The Golden Days of Sail

Some of the most beautiful ships in the whole history of seafaring were the clippers. Here is a painting of one of them, the *Anglesey*, approaching harbour under full sail, in about the year 1850.

By the nineteenth century, world trade was booming as never before. Several European nations had large empires from which they obtained raw materials for industry, and foodstuffs. The United States, too, was growing into a great trading nation. Merchants in these countries rivalled each other to get their goods transported across the high seas and to their customers in the shortest possible time. They relied on the clippers and their crews to do this for them.

'Clipping the Wind'

The word clipper comes from the expression 'to clip the wind', meaning to use the wind to the best advantage. To do this the clippers carried the greatest possible area of sail, in relation to their size and weight. And with their complex rigging, the sails could catch the wind at just the right angle. Though they were merchantmen, designed to carry cargo, the clippers' hulls were long and sleek, like large racing yachts.

One of the most profitable trades they handled was tea from China and India to Britain. Another was wool from Australia to Europe and the United States. The celebrated *Cutty Sark*, now preserved in dry dock beside the Thames at Greenwich, engaged mainly in the wool trade. American clippers — some of the largest — also carried gold-hungry passengers from New York and Boston right round the tip of South America (Cape Horn) and up to San Francisco on the Pacific coast during the Californian gold rush of the 1850s.

The clippers operated on what for those days were record-breaking schedules: Hong Kong to London in 90 days; Melbourne to Liverpool in 63 days; Boston to Liverpool in 14 days. Given favourable winds and currents a clipper could cover up to 640 kilometres (400 miles) in a 24-hour period. Racing against time, and sometimes against each other, clipper captains took many risks, driving their ships on through storms till they were in danger of capsizing, and urging their crews to the point of exhaustion.

Steamships

The clippers were the most exciting and glamorous ships afloat. But take another look at the picture. To the left of our clipper is a steamship.

In 1818, the American ship *Savannah* made a crossing of the Atlantic under combined sail and steam power. In 1838 another ship, *Sirius*, managed the same crossing under steam power alone. For another fifty years, most new ocean-going ships combined sail and steam. But by the end of the nineteenth century, the steamship had taken over completely, and the clippers had passed into history.

The Age of Steam

This is a painting of the opening of the Stockton and Darlington Railway in 1825. A newspaper of the day described the event: 'Horsemen galloping across the fields to accompany the engine, and the people on foot running on each side of the road, endeavouring in vain to keep up with the cavalcade . . . In some parts the speed was frequently twelve miles per hour and in one place, for a short distance, fifteen miles per hour.'

There had been 'railways' of a kind before this: horses, and then stationary steam engines equipped with long cables, that hauled trucks along wooden or iron sets of rails, usually carrying coal away from a mine. Then in 1808 Richard Trevithick built one of the first steam locomotives to run on rails — the *Catch Me Who Can*, which he exhibited on a circular track near the present Euston station in London. Another very early rail steam locomotive, built to work at a colliery, was *Puffing Billy*.

Locomotion and Rocket

But with the Stockton and Darlington, the railway age had truly begun. The locomotive in our picture is *Locomotion*, designed and built by George Stephenson. Perhaps more important than the speed it attained was the amount of freight it could haul — nearly ninety tonnes.

Stephenson quickly followed this achievement with the even more famous *Rocket*. At the Rainhill locomotive trials near Liverpool, in 1829, *Rocket* amazed the world by reaching a speed of just over 48 km/h (30 m.p.h.). Nobody, and no vehicle, had ever moved as fast before. Some doctors warned that at such speeds people's lungs might burst!

Building the Railways

Despite such warnings, and some serious accidents, nothing could stop the spread of the railways. In Britain, engineers George Stephenson and his son Robert, Isambard Kingdom Brunel and others, spanned rivers and valleys with massive iron bridges or stone viaducts, drove tunnels through hills and mountains, as they criss-crossed the land with their 'iron roads'. By 1850 there were over 11,000 kilometres (7,000 miles) of track throughout the British Isles. Gustav Eiffel in France was another great engineer of the new railway age.

The railways were a marvellous new form of transport. Trucks and coaches ran much more efficiently on metal tracks than on roads, because there was less friction between wheels and track. Steam locomotives provided more power, speed and endurance than anything previously known. Passengers could travel from place to place in a fraction of the time previously taken by stage coach. Huge loads of coal, timber and manufactured goods could be transported in as many hours as it had previously taken days or even weeks by road, barge or sailing ship.

Balloons and Airships

This picture shows the first British balloon ascent made by James Sadler and a friend, above the rooftops of Oxford in 1810.

The First Air Travellers

At Annonay in France in June 1783, the brothers Joseph and Étienne Montgolfier had already sent aloft the first hot-air balloon — so called because it was made to rise by the hot air from a fire lit beneath it. In November 1783, Pilâtre de Rozier and the Marquis d'Arlande took off in a second Montgolfier hot-air balloon, sailing high over the rooftops of Paris for about 12 kilometres (7 miles) — the first air travellers — until the air in the big, splendidly decorated balloon cooled down and it drifted back to earth.

France continued to make ballooning history. Still in 1783, Jacques Charles demonstrated a different type of balloon, one filled with the lighter-than-air gas, hydrogen. Two years later, Jean-Pierre Blanchard made the first airborne crossing of the Channel from Dover to Calais, in his own hydrogen balloon.

Balloons had their true hour of glory in 1870, when Paris was besieged during the Franco-Prussian War. Dozens were used to air-lift people out of the beleaguered city.

But balloon travel was a risky business, since the balloon itself was almost impossible to control. Another Frenchman, Henri Giffard, in 1852, overcame this problem with a much improved type of balloon called a 'dirigible'. This had a cigar-shaped gas bag, beneath which was suspended a platform holding a small steam engine and propeller. In it he made a powered flight of 27 kilometres (17 miles).

Airships

Other, larger dirigibles led, in 1900, to the first true passenger-carrying airship, designed by Germany's Graf von Zeppelin. This had a rigid-framed gas container, about 140 metres (440 feet) long, which was filled or emptied as required; and was powered by petrol engines driving propellers.

During the First World War, 'Zeppelins' were used to bomb England. After the war, Germany, Britain and Italy all built still larger airships able to carry up to 50 passengers comfortably, at speeds of 160 km/h (100 m.p.h.).

Most spectacular of all was the German airship *Hindenburg*. The gas container was 254 metres (800 feet) long, and she could fly at speeds of up to 290 km/h (180 m.p.h.). But in 1937, while moored to her mast near New York, the *Hindenburg* suddenly burst into flames and crashed, killing her passengers and crew. This followed several other airship disasters, caused by the difficulty of handling them in storms, and by the inflammable hydrogen gas.

The great days of the airships were over, leaving the skies to the growing fleets of airliners we shall read about on page 45.

The First Cars

The birth of the motor car: a contemporary print of the motorized tricycle designed by Karl Benz in 1888. The engine is mounted behind the passenger seats. The rear wheels are driven by chains. Maximum speed was 15 km/h (9 m.p.h.).

'Horseless Carriages'

The famous German inventor was by no means the first to build a mechanized road vehicle. As long ago as 1770, Frenchman Nicholas Cugnot built a strange-looking steam car that managed a speed of about 5 km/h (3 m.p.h.) for periods of up to twenty minutes at a time. In the early years of the nineteenth century, two Englishmen, Richard Trevithick and Goldsworthy Gurney, built steam carriages. And in 1860, another Frenchman, Étienne Lenoir, designed a vehicle with an engine that ran on coal gas. But the significant feature of Benz's vehicle was its petrol engine. It was this that pointed the way forward for road transport.

The onlookers in our picture all appear very relaxed and happy. The driver himself, his lady passengers, and the dog, look as though they haven't a care in the world. In reality, early motor vehicles — 'horseless carriages' as they were called — alarmed most people. In Britain, they were at first forbidden to drive along a public highway at more than 6.5 km/h (4 m.p.h.) — even less in towns — and had to be preceded by a man on foot waving a red warning flag! The repeal of this law in 1896 was celebrated by a special run from London to Brighton, now a famous annual event for veteran cars (those built before 1919).

Like many new inventions, early motor cars themselves were unreliable. They frequently broke down, so inspiring a popular song 'Get Out and Get Under', referring to the driver on his back under the car, trying to repair the engine.

Popular Motoring

But this state of affairs soon changed. Motor vehicles played a big part in the First World War. Paris taxi cabs, for example, were used to rush troops to the Front in the Battle of the Marne in 1914. Many more motor vehicles were ambulances, to take the wounded away from the battle zones.

Luxury motoring reached its peak after the war. Long, sleek automobiles with glamorous names like Delage, Hispano-Suiza, Lagonda, Isotta-Fraschini, Duesenberg, not to mention Rolls-Royce and Bentley, Daimler and Mercedes-Benz, cruised along the roads, often with a liveried chauffeur at the wheel.

But motoring was no longer the exclusive pleasure of the very rich. Before the First World War, Henry Ford in the United States had already launched his automobile named the 'Model T', one of the first examples of industrial mass production. By 1927 over 15 million Model T Fords were on the roads. The age of popular motoring had begun.

Trans-continental Railways

This wintry scene on an American railroad in about 1875 shows that an avalanche has blocked the track. The big locomotive headlamp attached to the smoke stack shines out into the cold, dark night. The wide smoke stack was designed to catch flying sparks, at a time when most American locomotives burnt wood rather than coal. The 'cowcatcher' in front cleared the track of obstacles in the days when trains often traversed wild and open countryside.

Building the Railroads

The building of the railroads was one of the most dramatic chapters in America's history. In 1862, President Lincoln gave the go-ahead for construction of a line to complete the 4,800-kilometre (3,000-mile) rail link from coast to coast. Two railroad companies, the Union Pacific and the Central Pacific, started laying track from opposite directions.

The construction gangs had to bring all their own stores and equipment as they advanced over uncharted territory: prairies, barren deserts, and the towering Rocky Mountains. They faced floods, blizzards, burning heat, and Red Indian attacks. Fourteen years were scheduled for the task: it was finished in six. The two lines met at Promontory Point, Utah; and at a special ceremony on 10 May 1869, the last rivet — made of gold — was driven in.

An even greater distance was covered by the Trans-Siberian Railway, opened in 1900. It linked Moscow with the Pacific port of Vladivostok, across some 6,500 kilometres (4,000 miles) of trackless forest and half-frozen scrub. In Australia, track was laid dead straight for over 480 kilometres (300 miles) across the flat, sun-scorched Nullarbor ('Treeless') Plain.

Very long, heavy trains operated over such routes, between towns often 500 kilometres (300 miles) apart, and some enormous steam locomotives were built to haul them. One American model named 'Big Boy' had two sets of cylinders, sixteen driving wheels, and weighed (without its tender) 350 tonnes.

Passenger Comfort

Passengers making long trans-continental journeys needed extra comforts too. The United States pioneered improvements in passenger travel. American coaches were the first to be built with central corridors, so that passengers could use washrooms and lavatories on the move.

George Pullman, in 1865, introduced refreshment and sleeping cars, and a Belgian, Georges Nagelmackers, copied his idea, hiring out luxurious dining cars and 'wagons-lits' to long-distance European trains, like the famous 'Orient Express'.

Before the First World War, the 'Trans-Siberian Express' took nine days to make the journey between Moscow and Vladivostok. It carried dining and sleeping cars, bathrooms, gymnasium and saloon with piano.

Trams and Buses

Drama in a Paris street! A steam tram has come off the rails and has careered down the road, knocking over a pedestrian and overturning a carriage, before crashing into a tree. Happily, such accidents have been rare. Trams and buses — the two basic types of public transport in towns and cities — have a good safety record.

'Tram' is an old Scandinavian word that once described the wooden planks used to form a track for carts and trucks. One of the first tramways or 'street car' systems was opened in New York in 1832, at a time when American roads, even in towns, were still very bad, and vehicles running on rails offered a much smoother ride than any other forms of road transport.

Horse-drawn Power

These early horse-drawn trams, both in America and in Europe, ran on raised tracks, like an ordinary railway. When these proved to be a hazard in busy streets, tracks were sunk into the roadway, level with the surface, to form the more familiar tram lines.

'Bus' is short for the Latin 'omnibus', meaning 'for all'; and like trams, the first models were drawn by horses. An early development was double-decker trams and buses — an idea prompted in the first instance by the fact that people often clambered on to the roofs of the old single-deckers, hoping for a free ride! Passengers on the new top decks sat back to back on two long rows of wooden seats, an arrangement which was known as 'knife-board' seating.

Mechanized Transport

During the nineteenth century, some trams were given steam traction (like the one in our picture); but most were fitted with the newly-invented electric motor, and took their power from overhead cables by a special type of arm with a little wheel, called a trolley. Most buses, by contrast, changed from being drawn by horses straight over to petrol or diesel engines.

Both buses and trams made a big impact on city life. London's fleet of red buses has for long been a tradition in the city. San Francisco's cable-car trams, which ply up and down the town's steep hills, have been a favourite form of transport for well over a century.

In general, buses have won out over trams because they do not need tracks or power lines. Today, many buses also operate over distances that were once covered only by railway trains. America's famous 'Greyhound' buses carry passengers in speed and comfort to destinations right across the continent. In Europe, too, bus services operate in rural areas and link most of the towns and cities, and in many countries of Asia, they are an important and cheap form of transport.

Flying Machines

This artist's impression shows the brothers Orville and Wilbur Wright testing one of their flying machines over Kitty Hawk Sands, North Carolina, USA. A few months later, in a modified version of it, they made the world's first 'powered, sustained and controlled flight.' The date was 17 December 1903.

This was true flying, as distinct from the ballooning we read about on page 31. The propellers, driven by a piston petrol engine, drew the aircraft forward. The air moving over the wings gave it sufficient lift to leave the ground. Once this secret of aeronautics had been discovered, events moved fast.

The Wright Brothers made several flights at Kitty Hawk, the longest of 260 metres (852 feet) lasting 59 seconds. Two years later, at Dayton, Ohio, they were airborne for 38 minutes. In 1909, the Frenchman Louis Blériot, flew the 38 kilometres (23 miles) across the Channel from Calais to Dover in 37 minutes.

During the First World War, aircraft were used for reconnaissance, aerial combat, and even on bombing missions.

Epic Flights

In 1919, two British aviators, John Alcock and Arthur Brown, made the first flight across the Atlantic, from Newfoundland to Ireland, in a Vickers Vimy bomber fitted with extra fuel tanks. During their epic flight of 16 hours 27 minutes, Brown had to clamber out on to the wings to chip off ice.

Other historic flights include the American Charles Lindbergh's first solo flight across the Atlantic in *Spirit of St Louis*. In 1930, Britain's Amy Johnson flew solo, with stops for refuelling, from London to Australia in just over 19 days; and in 1936 and '37, New Zealander Jean Batten completed solo flights from Britain to New Zealand, and Australia to Britain, in 11 days and under 6 days respectively.

Passenger Services

By then, aviation was no longer just for a few intrepid flyers. The first regular air mail and passenger service had opened between London and Paris in 1919. Aircraft grew rapidly in size and power — all-metal, four-engined machines carried thirty or more passengers at speeds of over 160 km/h (100 m.p.h.), with a range of more than 1,000 kilometres (620 miles). Some used runways — others, very popular with passengers, were 'flying boats' that took off and landed on water.

One of the first commercial airports was at Croydon, near London — headquarters of British Imperial Airways, that operated flights to South Africa, India, Australia and other parts of the then British Empire and Commonwealth.

During the 1920s and '30s, many other nations established international airlines. Although air travel was still far too expensive for most people, it was already becoming big business.

Ocean Liners

This painting of the majestic *Mauretania* shows her steaming up Scotland's Firth of Forth. Behind her, a steam train crosses the mighty Forth Bridge.

As we have read on page 27, the change from sailing to steam ships took place during the nineteenth century. In 1840, the Canadian Samuel Cunard began a regular mail service between Britain and North America, with his paddle steamer *Britannia*. This ship made the Atlantic crossing from Liverpool to Halifax, Nova Scotia, and on to Boston, in 14 days.

The First Steamships

In 1854, I.K. Brunel built his colossal *Great Eastern*. This, too, was a paddle steamer with sails, like all ships at that time. But she also had an iron hull and experimental screw propellers, setting the pattern for future steamship development.

By the beginning of this century, ocean liners were operating on all the world's major sea routes. The route that attracted most attention, because of the number of passengers who used it, was the Atlantic crossing between Europe and the U.S.A.

In 1907 the Cunard company launched the *Mauretania* — the four-funnelled giant in our picture — which gained the coveted 'Blue Riband' award for the fastest crossing, with speeds of over 27 knots. Five years later came the 46,328-ton *Titanic*, the largest ship afloat, and supposedly unsinkable on account of her water-tight compartments. Tragically, she struck an iceberg on her maiden voyage to America and sank with many of her passengers and crew.

Ocean Rivalry

This disaster did not stop the big shipping companies competing against each other to build even bigger, faster, more luxurious liners for the North Atlantic route. Soon after the First World War came the German liner *Bremen*. Then in 1935 and 1936 came the two greatest rivals, the French-built *Normandie* and Cunard's *Queen Mary*. The *Normandie* was perhaps the most luxurious of all, with her indoor swimming pools, cinema, dance hall, and enormous first-class dining room lined with glass.

Just before the Second World War, the *Queen Elizabeth* was launched. During the war she served as a troopship, then resumed her role as a passenger liner. In the 1950s, America's *United States* became the grandest, fastest liner on the North Atlantic run, averaging speeds of nearly 36 knots, and a crossing time of well under four days.

She was almost the last of the great liners. Jet aircraft were now cutting travelling times from weeks to hours. The few liners still left, like the *Queen Elizabeth II (QE2)*, now take passengers on luxury cruises.

Today's great ships are the oil tankers, monsters of up to 500,000 tonnes, transporting the fuel that everyone needs.

Underground Travel

Look at the chandeliers and ornately decorated roof in this station on the Moscow Underground, or Metro. When it was being planned, the Soviet government wanted to give ordinary people a taste of the luxury enjoyed by the Tsar and his court before the Revolution in 1917. So the stations were built to look like palaces.

The history of underground railways goes back to the last century, when congestion in the streets of large cities was already a problem. Running trams or trains under the streets was a good way of relieving it.

The London Underground

The world's first stretch of underground railway was opened in London in 1863. Named the Metropolitan Line (from which other systems were to take the shortened name of 'Metro'), it originally had open coaches and steam locomotives. Travelling on it was a noisy, dirty business, but it proved very popular, and was soon carrying more than 26,000 passengers a day.

The Metropolitan Line was constructed by what is called the 'cut-and-cover' process — digging a wide trench along the street for the tracks and stations, then covering it over again. But London soon had much deeper underground lines. The method for these was to sink shafts into the ground and then burrow through the earth. This was done with the aid of a large circular iron 'shield'. As workmen dug through the London clay, so the shield was pushed forward, inch by inch. The tunnels were then lined with curved cast-iron plates, so forming a long tube. The very first section of London 'tube' line, opened in 1870, had cable cars. The first 'tube' line with electric trains, opened in 1890, ran under the Thames, linking the City with parts of South London.

City 'Metros'

Other big cities followed London's lead; Paris in 1900, New York in 1904. The London Underground system still has the longest amount of track (over 380 kilometres/240 miles); but the New York Subway has the most stations (461); while the Moscow Metro carries the most passengers (over 2,000 million a year).

Today over fifty other towns and cities around the world have underground systems and more are planned. Existing underground railways are constantly being improved: the Paris Metro, for example, now has trains that run on pneumatic tyres, so giving them faster acceleration, better braking, and reducing noise.

Some cities, notably New York and Chicago in the United States, and Liverpool in England, once had trains running over the streets instead of under them. Such 'elevated' railways have not been as popular as underground ones. But Wuppertal in West Germany has for long had an unusual form of transport, consisting of coaches slung beneath a type of overhead monorail that runs through the town.

The Motor Age

This photograph shows a present-day traffic intersection in Tokyo. Notice that nearly all the vehicles are private cars. There are plenty of buses, trucks, motor- and pedal-cycles on the roads today, but it is the private car that has revolutionized road transport in this century.

As we read on page 33, there were already millions of cars on the roads before the Second World War. In the 1930s, in America and in Germany, 'freeways' or 'autobahnen' — different names for motorways — were being built. Traffic lights were also invented to control traffic at busy junctions.

The Car Boom

After the war, car production was soon booming as never before. Between 1950 and 1970 the number of vehicles on Britain's roads shot up from 4 to 15 million. In Japan the increase was even more dramatic: from under a million to 18 million.

To accommodate such huge growth rates, most countries have followed America's and Germany's lead with the construction of motorways — long, winding ribbons of multi-lane highways passing over, under and round each other, keeping the traffic moving non-stop between towns and cities.

Motorways can sometimes get congested, but traffic congestion in towns and cities is a major problem of our times. Various schemes have been used to try to cope with it. Sets of traffic lights are co-ordinated to regulate the movement of big city traffic. One-way street systems keep traffic moving in a single direction only. There are multi-storey car parks, and parking meters, to try to keep streets clear of stationary vehicles.

And there are other problems. Thousands of motor vehicles concentrated in a small area create high levels of pollution from their petrol and diesel engine exhausts. Accident rates are also high, where cars, buses, cyclists and pedestrians are all crowded into the same city streets.

Solving the Problems

Traffic experts and town planners are trying to solve these urgent problems. They point out that a single bus can carry as many passengers as forty or fifty individual cars, and suggest that private vehicles should be banned from city centres.

Motor manufacturers are being encouraged to produce small, electric-driven run-about cars that would take up much less road space and cut down on pollution in the cities. More underground railways are proposed with big car parks at stations in the suburbs, for people to leave their cars and travel on into the city by train. Another idea is moving pavements, that could carry people along the streets and do away with city traffic altogether!

Private cars are now the most widely-used form of transport in countries of the West, but they continue to present many problems which have yet to be solved.

46

Speeding through the Skies

An American-built DC-10 jet airliner of West Germany's Lufthansa airline flies high above the snowy peaks of the Alps.

As we read on page 39, air travel was already important before the Second World War. During the war, as a result of experimental work by Britain's Frank Whittle and Germany's Ernst Heinkel, jet fighters came into service, far outstripping in speed and power any propeller aircraft.

Jet Aircraft

Jet propulsion is based on the law of physics stating that every action or thrust produces an equal and opposite reaction or thrust. In a jet engine fuel is burnt and the hot gases of this combustion are blown out at the back. The engine, and the aircraft it is driving, moves forward with an equivalent force.

The big change in civil aviation from propeller to jet aircraft began in 1952, when the de Havilland *Comet 1* entered service with the British Overseas Airways Corporation. With four jet engines, giving it a 'cruising', or average, speed of 780 km/h (490 m.p.h.), the aircraft was twice as fast as any existing propeller-driven airliner.

Comet 1 had several bad accidents and was withdrawn. But other jet airliners were soon on the scene. The American Boeing 707, with four jet engine 'pods' slung under the swept-back wings, had the fastest speed, longest range and biggest passenger-carrying capacity of any airliner yet. The French-built *Caravelle* (named after the old sailing ships described on page 13), had two jet engines mounted by the tail plane. The first 'generation' of jet airliners were nearly all based on one or other of these designs.

Air Travel for All

All this time, the number of airline passengers was growing by leaps and bounds. From 1950 to 1966, the total rose from around 30 million passengers a year to over 200 million a year.

To meet this huge increase in air travel, the Boeing company built their 747 'Jumbo' jet. This carries up to 500 passengers, plus all their luggage, at a cruising speed of over 900 km/h (600 m.p.h.), and with a range of over 9,600 kilometres (6,000 miles). The aircraft includes a double-deck and a lounge bar for first-class passengers.

Air travel has also gone 'supersonic' (faster than the speed of sound), with the *Concorde* built jointly by Britain and France, and the Soviet Union's Tupolev 144. The two 'delta wing' aircraft have cruising speeds of around 2,400 km/h (1,500 m.p.h.), or Mach 2 — twice the speed of sound.

Today a staggering 400 million people a year travel by air. International airports like Chicago O'Hare, New York Kennedy, London Heathrow and Paris Orly, are as big as whole towns. All this has happened a mere eighty years after the Wright brothers first took to the air in their fragile craft.

Speeding over Land

A French Railways' TGV ('Train Grand Vitesse' or High-Speed Train) leaving Paris on its journey south to the Mediterranean. These electric trains run at speeds of up to 300 km/h (nearly 190 m.p.h.).

Thanks to a plentiful supply of hydro-electric power from the Alps, Switzerland was one of the first countries to switch from steam to electric locomotives on its railways, as long ago as 1910. During the 1920s, the British Southern Railway company electrified its London suburban services and main lines to the south coast.

French Railways (SNCF) forged ahead with electrification after the Second World War. In 1955 one of their electric locomotives achieved a new rail speed record of 432 km/h (205 m.p.h.). Similar locomotives hauled the Paris-Marseilles-Riviera *Mistral* Express, for many years one of the world's fastest and most comfortable trains.

Japanese Pioneers

The TGV in our photograph marks the latest advance in passenger train design — pioneered by the Japanese when they opened their specially-built Tokaido Line from Tokyo to Osaka in 1964. There is no separate locomotive on such trains. The power units and coaches are constructed as completely self-contained multiple-unit trains. Thus they can operate back and forth with the least delay and inconvenience; and

because of the way the compartment sections are linked, they travel safely round curves at the same high speed.

Other fast, multiple-unit passenger trains, such as those running on British Rail, have diesel engines instead of electric motors. Today, diesel-powered trains and loco-motives, running on fuel oil, operate all over the world, where lines have not been electrified. Only a few countries, including China, still have steam locomotives in service.

Freight Containers

Railway freight services have also advanced in recent years. Fleets of wagons take standardized 'containers', which can be transferred quickly and easily from ship to road or rail. In many countries, railways operate container freight trains that run to and fro almost like conveyor belts.

Railways have even more exciting plans for the future. In fact, railways as we know them may soon be a thing of the past. Britain, the United States, West Germany and France are among the countries experimenting with monorail (single rail) trains. These will not run on wheels, but glide over the rail, powered by new technology such as electro-magnetic propulsion. Trains like this, virtually free from friction, could easily travel at speeds of 400 km/h (250 m.p.h.). They could also be remote-controlled by computers, which would see the end of elaborate and costly signalling systems.

Hovercraft and Helicopters

Hovercraft are among the most recent additions to our forms of transport. The one in our photograph is about to glide off its apron of land and begin its journey over the water.

Skimming over Water

The hovercraft, or ACV (air-cushioned vehicle), was invented by British engineer Christopher Cockerell. Air blown downwards from the body or fuselage is contained by a strong rubber 'skirt', so creating a 'cushion' of air that raises the hovercraft above whatever surface it has been resting on. The vehicle can then be driven either by propellers, like the one in our picture, or by jet propulsion. With no wheels, or hull in contact with the water, it is a very efficient vehicle.

The first commercial hovercraft service, between Gosport on the English south coast and the Isle of Wight, was opened in 1965. Today hovercraft carry over 200 passengers and their cars at speeds of 80 km/h (50 m.p.h.) across the Channel between Britain and France; and other versions are operating car ferries across rivers, large lakes and short sea passages all around the world. Even more powerful models might one day skim at speed across oceans and deserts.

The hovercraft's only drawback is that it cannot travel over very rough water or rugged or uneven terrain. But this is no problem for another important form of modern transport — the helicopter.

Hovering over Land

'Helicopter' comes from the Greek 'helix', meaning 'spiral' or 'screw'. Four hundred years ago Leonardo da Vinci wrote of a flying machine that could 'screw itself up in the air and rise high'. But it was not until the 1930s that a few pioneers, notably the Russian-American Igor Sikorsky, began to build the first successful helicopters. These had a large horizontal rotor for lift and a smaller vertically-placed one to steady the fuselage.

Their development was speeded up during the Second World War, since a flying machine that needed no runway, could hover over enemy positions, and help in land or sea rescue operations was of great military value. The biggest ones today, with several rotors, can lift loads weighing up to 40,000 kilograms (88,000 lbs). Smaller machines are ideal in all sorts of situations, from emergency rescue operations to police surveillance.

Helicopters are a type of VTOL machine (Vertical Take-off and Landing). So are 'jet-lift' machines that raise themselves by jet thrust from below rather than by rotors from above.

The first VTOL of this type, with no wings and no propellers, built in 1954, was nicknamed the 'Flying Bedstead'. Today, some VTOL aircraft have jet engines that apply downward thrust for take-off and then adjust their position for normal forward flight.

'Road Trains'

One of the largest road transport units in the world is this Australian 'Road Train'. The massive diesel-engined 'tractor' hauls a string of huge tankers or trailers across the Australian continent. This one operates between Adelaide, in South Australia, and Darwin in the north — a distance of 3,200 kilometres (2000 miles) across the heart of Australia's vast 'outback'.

The history of modern road haulage goes back little further than that of the aeroplane. Before about 1750, as we have read, roads everywhere were so bad that people much preferred to use rivers, or small coastal ships as a means of transporting goods from one part of a country to another. Then came canals, and after them railways, to handle cross-country goods. Road haulage did not really get going until this century.

Railway companies were among the first to introduce it. Their road vans carried goods to and from railway depots and individual customers. By the 1930s, however, big diesel-engine lorries and trucks were being built and road haulage companies were operating over long-distance routes in direct competition with the railways.

Trucks and Lorries

The break-through came in the 1960s, with the introduction of large articulated trucks and lorries — a 'tractor unit' attached to one or more trailers, allowing the whole long vehicle to negotiate bends and corners easily. Their great advantage over railways was that they could go practically anywhere, racing along trunk roads and motorways, or nosing their way through city streets to factories and shops. Soon they were handling over seventy per cent of goods transported around the world.

Today's articulated trucks have many functions. Tankers carry milk, wine, beer and chemicals for industry, and petrol and diesel fuel for road users. Refrigerator vans carry perishable foods. Others are specially designed, to carry standard-sized containers, and operate mainly between ports and factories.

Juggernauts

These large, heavy vehicles are sometimes called juggernauts — a Hindu word meaning something that crushes everything else in its path! Juggernauts can disturb the comfort of people living near roads which are used by them, and they are banned from certain routes.

Our mighty Australian 'Road Train', however, is only likely to disturb a few kangaroos and dingoes, as it rumbles on over the empty scrub. Interestingly, for part of the way between Adelaide and Darwin, it follows one of the old camel routes. Camels were imported to Australia when much of the continent was still a trackless waste, and caravans like those described on page 15 were the most practical means of transport for the pioneers.

Travelling in Space

With a shattering roar and a sheet of white-hot exhaust, a rocket rises from its launch-pad at Cape Kennedy, Florida, at the start of a space mission. Such a stupendous release of power is needed to lift the rocket and its pay-load out of Earth's atmosphere and project it into space.

Rockets, working on the same scientific principle as jet engines (see page 47) have been used, for fun and for war, since the Middle Ages. The one that opened the way to space travel was Germany's V2 (Revenge Weapon 2) that bombarded London during the Second World War. It rose vertically into the air from its launching pad, reaching a speed of 6,437 km/h (4,000 m.p.h.) and a height of nearly 90 kilometres (56 miles).

With the V2 as their model, the United States and the Soviet Union started their own rocket research and space programmes as soon as the war ended. Indeed, both super-powers grabbed as many of Germany's top scientists as they could, to help them.

First Men in Space
The Soviet Union at first took the lead. In 1957 they placed in orbit around the Earth *Sputnik 1* (the word means 'Little Traveller') — the very first man-made space satellite. In 1959 they sent their satellite *Lunik 3* right out of Earth's gravitational field and into orbit around the moon. And in April 1961 they scored their greatest triumph when cosmonaut Yuri Gagarin orbited Earth in his capsule — the first man in space.

America's President John F. Kennedy then announced that the United States was aiming to send a man to the moon by the end of the 1960s. On 20 July 1969, two American astronauts, Neil Armstrong and Edwin Aldrin, stepped down from their *Apollo* space capsule on to the dusty, lifeless surface of the moon.

Much else has been achieved in the short but dramatic history of space travel and exploration. Soviet cosmonauts and American astronauts have manned space laboratories, observing such phenomena as the sun's radiation.

To the Farthest Planets
In 1975 the Soviet Union sent a capsule 143 million kilometres (89 million miles) across space to dive through the surrounding carbon dioxide clouds and land on the oven-hot surface of the planet Venus. The next year, the Americans landed a space laboratory on the reddish-brown rock and sand of the planet Mars.

Another American space probe — *Voyager 2*, launched in 1977 — has radioed back to Earth pictures of the more distant planets — Jupiter (the largest) and Saturn (with its rings), and is scheduled to pass Uranus in 1986. Beyond lie the outermost planets of our solar system, Neptune and Pluto. Far, far beyond again — at a distance measured by the speed of light — is the next nearest star to our own sun.

Acknowledgements and Sources of Pictures

cover An early nineteenth-century painting of a Mississippi steamboat alongside the wharf. (Wayland Picture Library)

page 8 An ancient Egyptian mural showing Nile boats similar to those used by the Pharaoh Tutankhamun in about 1350 BC. (Mary Evans Picture Library)

page 10 A painting from a fifteenth-century illuminated manuscript, illustrated and handwritten by monks. (Wayland Picture Library)

page 12 A medieval illustration of an English army embarking across the Channel to fight the French in the Hundred Years War. (Wayland Picture Library)

page 14 A reproduction from an Arabian miniature, painted in 1236. (Mansell Collection)

page 16 War canoes of the Tahitian islanders, painted by William Hodges in 1769, when he visited Tahiti with Captain Cook. (National Maritime Museum)

page 18 *The Rocky Mountains: Emigrants Crossing the Plains*—a print by Currier and Ives, printmakers of the American way of life, 1866. (Peter Newark's Western Americana)

page 20 'A Midnight Race on the Mississippi' from a lithograph by Currier and Ives, 1860. (Peter Newark's Western Americana)

page 22 'The Mail Coach in a Thunder Storm on Newmarket Heath', painted by James Pollard in the mid-nineteenth century. (Wayland Picture Library)

page 24 A print from a nineteenth-century painting of Regent's Canal at the East entrance to Islington Tunnel. (Wayland Picture Library)

page 26 A Currier and Ives print of the Clipper *Anglesey*, of about 1850. (Wayland Picture Library)

page 28 'Opening of the Stockton and Darlington Railway 1825'—a painting by Terence Cuneo. (British Transport Museum)

page 30 'Ascent of James Sadler at Oxford 1810', a nineteenth-century print of the first British balloon flight. (Wayland Picture Library)

page 32 A print from a Leipzig newspaper of September 1888, illustrating an early Benz automobile. (Benz Museum)

page 34 A late nineteenth-century print of one of the first locomotives to cross the United States from coast to coast, from the Atlantic to the Pacific coast. (Mansell Collection)

page 36 A runaway tram in Paris in the early twentieth century. This picture originally appeared in the French magazine *Petit Parisien*, in 1900. (Mary Evans Picture Library)

page 38 'Orville Wright piloting a new aeroplane at Kitty-Hawk, North Carolina'. Printed in a French magazine of 1903. (Mansell Collection)

page 40 The *Mauretania*, painted in about 1935. An illustration in the *Queen Mary Souvenir Book*. (Mary Evans Picture Library)

page 42 A photograph of a station on the Moscow Metro. (Photographed by E. Ryabko-Minkin)

Sources of Further Information

PLACES TO VISIT

Bluebell Railway, Sheffield Park, Sussex. A working steam railway with steam era stations.

British Commercial Vehicle Museum, Preston, Lancs. Illustrates history of commercial vehicles from horse-drawn to the present.

Darlington Railway Museum, Yorkshire. Exhibits original Stockton and Darlington Railway, including *Locomotion*.

Donington Collection, Castle Donington, Derby. World's largest collection of grand-prix racing cars.

Doune Motor Museum, Perthshire. Unique display of vintage cars.

London Transport Museum, Covent Garden, London. Exhibition of buses, trams, trolley buses and railways.

Mark Hall Cycle Museum, Harlow, Essex. Collection of cycles from 1818 'Hobby Horse' to present.

Museum of Flight, North Berwick, near Edinburgh. Collection of aircraft from 1930 to modern jets.

National Maritime Museum, Greenwich, London. Many aspects of maritime history; also clipper *Cutty Sark* nearby.

National Motor Museum, Beaulieu, Hampshire. Exhibition of cars, showing the story of motoring.

National Railway Museum, York. Collections showing history and development of railway engineering.

National Tramway Museum, Crick, near Matlock. Unique collection of horse, steam and electric trams.

Nottingham Canal Museum, Nottingham. Displays of canal and river transport through the ages.

Science Museum, Kensington, London. Exhibitions showing development of transport and commerce.

Stratford-upon-Avon Motor Museum, Warwickshire. Unique collection of exotic vintage cars.

BOOKS

Ash, Russell, *The Wright Brothers* (Wayland, 1978)

Benson, D. S., *Man and the Wheel* (Priory Press, 1973)

Booth, G., *Buses* (Wayland, 1982)

Burgess Wise, David, *The Motor Car: An Illustrated International History* (Orbis Publishing, 1977)

Coleman, Terry, *The Liners: A History of the North Atlantic Crossing* (Allen Lane, 1976)

Embleton, G. A., *Passenger Aircraft* (Wayland, 1982)

Freeman Allan, G., *Trains* (Wayland, 1982)

Gatland, Kenneth, *The Illustrated Encyclopedia of Space Technology* (Salamander Books, 1981)

Grant, Neil, *Stagecoaches* (Kestrel, 1977)

Mondey, David (Ed.) *Aviation: The Complete Book of Aircraft and Flight* (Octopus Books, 1980)

Posthumus, Cyril, *Motor Cars* (Wayland, 1982)

Rowland, John, *The Automobile Man: The Story of Henry Ford* (Lutterworth, 1979)

Serling, Robert J., *The Jet Age* (Time Life Books, 1982)

Stuart, Richard H. (Ed.), *The Pictorial Story of Ships* (New English Library, 1977)

Tapper, Oliver, *The World's Great Pioneer Flights* (Bodley Head, 1975)

Young, Warren R., *The Helicopters* (Time Life, 1982)

Glossary

Aeronautics: The study or practice of flight.

Aqueduct: A bridge carrying a canal across a valley

Bireme: An ancient galley, or boat, with two banks of oars.

Caravan: A group of travellers with a train of camels, journeying through the desert.

Caravanserai: A public building for the shelter of camel caravans. It was constructed around a courtyard with an entrance large enough for loaded camels to enter.

Caravel: A two or three-masted sailing ship of the 15th and 16th centuries.

Carrack: A merchant ship of the 15th and 16th centuries.

Clipper: A fast sailing ship.

Cog: A sailing ship used for transport and commerce in the English Channel and North and Baltic seas, during the 13th and 14th centuries.

Dhow: An Arab sailing vessel with one or two masts.

Dirigible: A balloon or airship which can be steered or directed.

Felucca: A narrow sailing vessel used in the Mediterranean.

Hanseatic League: An association of towns in Northern Germany, formed to protect and control trade in the 14th and 15th centuries.

Hydroelectric power: Electricity generated by the pressure of falling water.

Hydrogen: A lighter-than-air gas which was used in early balloon flights.

Hieroglyphics: Ancient Egyptian writing which made use of picture symbols.

Juggernauts: Very large lorries for transporting goods by road.

Metro: The name for the underground railway system in certain cities, including Paris and Moscow.

Monorail: A single-track railway, often raised and with cars hanging from it.

Serf: A slave who worked on the land belonging to his owner.

Space satellite: A man-made object which is launched into space and put into orbit around the earth, moon or other planet. It can transmit scientific information to earth, or be used for communication.

Supersonic: Faster than the speed of sound.

Trek: A long, difficult journey, from the original journey made by the Boers with ox wagons.

Trireme: An ancient galley with three banks of oars.

Vikings: Pirates from northern Europe, who raided neighbouring coasts including Britain, during the years between the 8th to 11th centuries.

VTOL: Vertical take-off and landing—a type of hovercraft.

Wagons-lits: Sleeping cars on European railways.

Whirlicote: A medieval horse-drawn passenger wagon.

Index